CH00933324

ALL ABOUT LUNGEING

CONTENTS

Note Lunge training is designed for schooling the horse from the ground. Some of the techniques are unsuited to lungeing the rider on horseback.

2 • ALL ABOUT LUNGEING

When lungeing, as with riding, it must be remembered that the horse should be asked to go forward into all transitions, both upward and downward. In addition to a horse's normal work, you can lunge him 2–3 times a week. Avoid putting stress on his legs by not lungeing him beyond thirty minutes per session.

Every horse starts with the warming-up stage and should be lunged through the supple and loosen stage. He then progresses to basic lungeing (explained on pages 13-16) and once established, you can begin schooling him in balanced lungeing (see pages 17-23).

STARTING POINT

THE ASSESSMENT

Start to assess the horse by lungeing him from the cavesson; observe how he balances himself and note the following points. How is his neck set on to his shoulders? How does he balance himself in walk, trot and canter? Is each gait rhythmical? Does he hollow his back? Is he stiff? Is he strong? Powerful? Spooky or unflappable? Is he accepting the bit? How has he developed in his hindquarters, back, belly, loins and neck?

Accumulating this knowledge about a particular horse enables you to make

sensible decisions about lungeing him to the best advantage.

During the assessment focus on the main conformation points. For example, compare the examples of an old fashioned type of sports horse (top photograph) and the modern elite type of sports horse (below) with a head and neck set on well to his body and with good conformation.

EQUIPMENT

Cavesson A cavesson padded with soft leather prevents chafing. Ensure that the jowl strap is tightened sufficiently because this stops the cheek straps slipping over the horse's face and eyes. When lungeing a horse in a bridle and cavesson, fasten the cavesson straps under the bridle cheek pieces.

Be sympathetic to the horse and preserve the sensitivity of the horse's mouth by being aware of your own ability, so only clip the lunge rein to the bit ring when your hands are educated in the art of lungeing; until then fasten it to the cavesson.

Bridle Make sure the bridle fits comfortably. The noseband should sit snugly; a badly fitted noseband can cause a lot of discomfort. Measure the correct tightness for a drop or flash noseband by allowing two finger widths below the nose piece.

PAUL'S TIP

If lungeing from a cavesson, it is important to make sure the cavesson fits the horse well and comfortably.

Roller When using a roller, select one with at least three different D ring positions. Advice on how to use these D rings is given throughout the book.

Saddle A saddle can be used in place of a roller but stop the stirrups jangling against the horse's sides by wrapping each stirrup leather around each stirrup iron.

Boots and bandages Guard against injury to the horse's legs by using boots or bandages.

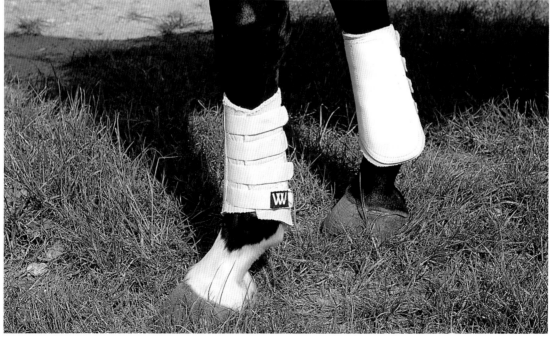

Lunge rein (right) Choose a lightweight, soft, cotton web rein which is approximately 6.5 m (21 ft) long.

Lunge whip (below left) This is normally 1.8 m (6 ft) long. The whip should handle easily and feel balanced and light in the hand.

Side reins (below right) Several types of side reins are available (see page 10 for more details).

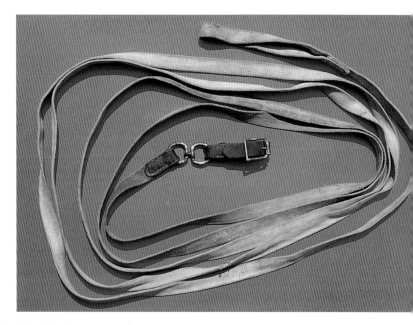

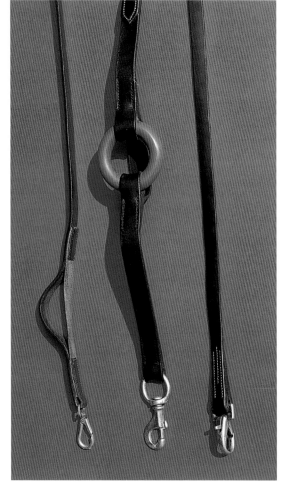

KEYS TO MOUTHING

THE MOUTH

To learn how to 'mouth' the horse, you must study his mouth. Observe the size and shape of his tongue and the corresponding size of his lower maxillary groove; the tongue rests in this groove. Are the bars of his mouth thinly covered or fleshy? Look at the size and shape of his lips.

Select a bit to suit the horse's mouth and he will learn to accept the bit willingly. Potential mouth and contact problems can, therefore, be avoided. The horse feels comfortable and happy to carry out your instructions and good behaviour becomes embedded in him. See page 9 for more details on bits.

THE GULLET

The gullet lies behind the jawbone. It runs like a furrow from the base of the ear to the bottom angle of the lower jaw. If there is a good angle to the gullet, the horse finds it easy to move his head vertically (i.e. bend his head from the poll) and laterally, (i.e. sideways) enabling him to achieve a high standard of flexion. This cannot be attained if the gullet has a tighter angle (see the photographs on the following page).

> **PAUL'S TIP**
>
> Teeth should be rasped every six months to a year. Ask your vet to remove any wolf teeth.

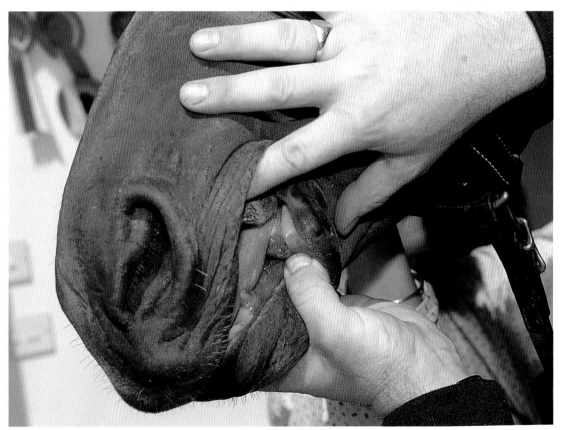

THREE TYPES OF SNAFFLES

Remember, the bit belongs to the horse's mouth not to your hands!

Observe how the horse does or does not accept the bit. For example, is he clamping the bit in his mouth or crossing his jaw to evade the action of the bit? Now select a bit from one of the three snaffle types listed below, one should suit the horse and help prevent any potential problems.

Standard type This type suits many horses. It includes the snaffles with cheeks, loose rings and eggbutts and can also include the French link, straight bar or jointed snaffles. The Fulmer bit, or snaffle with cheeks and keepers, holds the bit in a more 'set' position in the horse's mouth and gives an extra degree of flexion.

Horses not active in their gaits tend not to go to the bit nor take a supporting contact; they may need a thicker bit. Some horses appreciate the gentleness of the French-link snaffle. This mouth-friendly bit is jointed, but only to a small degree, and suits horses that resent the nutcracker action of a normal jointed bit.

A sensitive mouth needs a thick mouth-piece. A thinner bit has a sharper action and relays its message more clearly to less sensitive-mouthed horses.

Mouthing bit type Mouthing bits are fitted with keys which tickle the horse's tongue and persuade him to mouth the bit. The horse secretes saliva from his parotid gland when he mouths. These secretions bathe the bit and it is this effect that makes the bit mouth-friendly to the horse. The parotid gland, a salivary gland, lies within the gullet and begins at the root of the ear.

If you select a mouthing bit only use it for 4–5 days and then replace it with a copper snaffle.

Copper bit type Copper bits come in similar varieties to the standard type but the mouth piece is either partly or completely made of copper. Copper is reputed to be warmer in the horse's mouth than steel and encourages him to salivate.

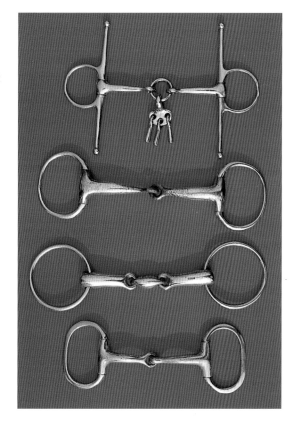

THE SIDE REINS

Side reins simulate the contact the rider takes on the reins and encourage the horse to seek the rein.

Side reins with elastic inserts have a lot of 'give' and are kind to a sensitive mouth. Side reins with rubber inserts 'give' less than the elastic variety and suit most horses. Fixed side reins have no 'give' and provide more control.

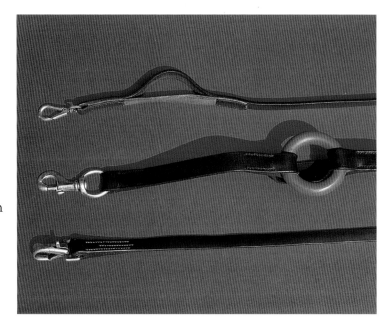

Length adjustment

Attach the clip end of the side reins to each bit ring. Loop the buckle either to a D ring on the roller, or through the girth straps of a saddle above the girth guard. Fasten the side reins so that the contact will be even on both sides of the bit by ensuring that both side reins are on the same hole number.

Double check that the reins are of the correct length. If you take hold of the reins behind the bit rings you should be able to take up at least a hand's measure of slack rein. Occasionally, check that leather side reins have not stretched.

PAUL'S TIP

Be careful not to tighten the side reins so that the horse's head is drawn back towards his body making him overbent. Err on the safe side, fit the side reins too long initially and only shorten them gradually until the horse's nose is just in front of the vertical.

Height adjustment Side reins are positioned lower on the roller for a young or inexperienced horse. It encourages him to stretch his head and neck to seek the contact with the bit, thus suppling his back and improving his gaits.

The time period for warming-up (the supple and loosen stage of each schooling session) differs according to the needs of each individual horse. As a general rule allow 10–15 minutes.

For warming-up the more experienced horse, position the side reins 15–23 cm (6–9 in) higher than for the inexperienced horse. Once the warm-up is completed, the horse progresses to the schooling stage of lungeing, balanced lungeing, and the side reins are now fastened to a higher D on the roller (see BALANCE LUNGEING on page 18).

The side reins are clipped onto the highest D rings for the developed horse. Normally this standard is reached when the horse can comfortably maintain more self-carriage over a reasonable period of time, i.e. at least 5–10 minutes (see PROMOTING BALANCE on page 17).

THREE LUNGE REIN TECHNIQUES

Ask the horse to take a constant, light contact on the lunge rein. Make sure there is a straight line from your hand and elbow to the horse's mouth.

Clip the lunge line to the bit. Lungeing from the bit closely simulates the rider's rein aids. You can fine tune the horse's understanding, and acceptance, of half halts by squeezing and releasing the lunge rein in the same way as you would with bridle reins. He should respond easily to your requests not being hampered by a rider's bodyweight.

Select the lunge rein technique that best suits the horse. You can, however, employ two methods together, for example, the normal control method on the left rein, and the indirect rein effect on the right rein.

Normal control This mode suits many horses. Fasten the lunge rein to the inside bit ring (see right).

More control This method gives more control over the exuberant horses. Run the lunge line through the inside bit ring, over the horse's head and attach the clip to the outside bit ring (see below, left).

Indirect rein control This helps to straighten the horse and is particularly useful when lungeing the horse on his hollow side, i.e. the side the horse naturally takes less of a contact with the bit.

Pass the lunge line through the inside bit ring and clip to the outside bit ring (below right).

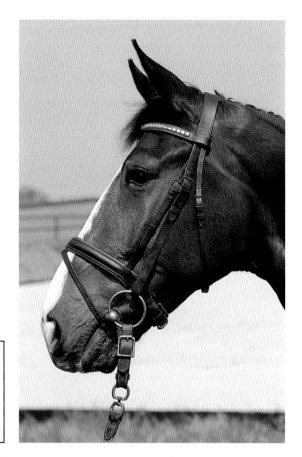

PAUL'S TIP

'Inside' refers to the side of the horse nearest to you and 'outside' refers to the side of the horse furthest away from you. This applies on both reins.

DIRECTING ENERGY AND BALANCE

These forces, used correctly, are important elements of successful lungeing. Horses are sensitive to body language. The way you position and move your body in relation to the horse's body communicates messages.

TRIANGLE OF CONTROL

Adopt the triangle of control. Assuming you are lungeing on the left rein, position your right shoulder level with the horse's quarters and your left shoulder level with his shoulders. This places you in a good position to effectively use the whip and, at the same time, maintain a straight line from your elbow through your hand and along the lunge rein to the horse's mouth. The triangle of control directs free forward movement: a) you are able to use the whip to ask for more energy;

b) you can half halt on the lunge rein to contain the energy and lighten the forehand; c) you can halt the horse by stepping forward slightly so that both of your shoulders are parallel to the horse's inside shoulder; d) if the horse is in good rhythm and balance, you can be passive with your aids and allow the horse to continue in self carriage.

If you lose the triangle of control, the horse can turn into the circle and lose his forward motion (see photo below).

THE LUNGE WHIP

The lunge whip manufactures energy in a similar way to the rider's leg aids.

Teach the horse to respect but not fear the whip. Stand by his shoulder and lightly touch his body with the lash or butt end of the whip.

Once he is confident and relaxed about this, the horse is ready to start work.

PAUL'S TIP

If you are inexperienced, follow the British Horse Society's recommendation and always wear a hard hat whilst lungeing.

Create activity by flicking the whip towards the horse's hind legs. Control the shoulders by flicking the whip towards his shoulders.

DEVELOPING RHYTHM

Develop an 'eye' for rhythm. Mark out four quadrants on a large circle, perhaps with bollards, and lunge the horse on this circle counting the number of strides he takes in each quadrant. The horse is moving in a regular rhythm when the strides between each bollard are of an equal number.

SUPPLE AND LOOSEN

A supple horse becomes resistance free and is more able and willing to please the rider. He moves forwards when you give the forward aids and responds to the retarding aids.

The horse's top line muscles (the muscles running from the tail, through the back and neck to the poll) are loosened and suppled if you allow him to stretch his head and neck to seek the bit: the horse goes to the bit. The horse can only engage his hindquarters more and move his hocks under his body, so lightening his forehand, when he is suppled and relaxed through these muscles.

The de Gogue Some horses carry their heads like peacocks and hollow their backs. Use the de Gogue to help such horses. It allows them more freedom than the side reins. They feel happier and less tense about stretching and looking for a supporting contact, this engages them so that they become more supple through their backs.

The de Gogue head piece fits under the head piece of the bridle.

Allow the horse's neck to stretch in a curve that is natural to him starting a hand's length in front of his wither. The neck should be stretched to its full length but not carried too high or too low.

PAUL'S TIP

Avoid pulling the horse's head into a shape, possibly frightening him or causing him to bring his head behind the vertical. Initially, fit the de Gogue loosely and only shorten the straps gradually.

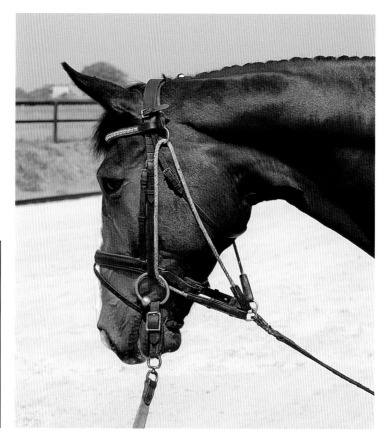

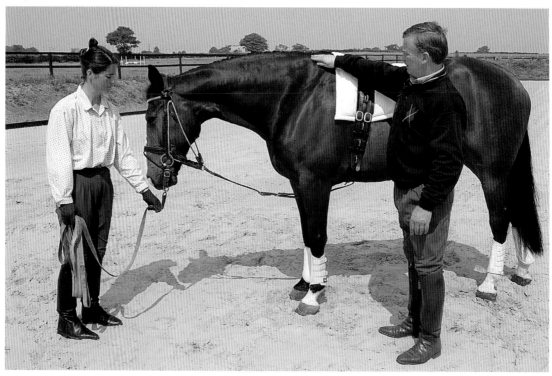

PROMOTING BALANCE

BALANCED LUNGEING

Balanced lungeing trains the horse in an advanced outline in the working or medium gaits. The horse works through his back, lifts his head and neck and automatically balances himself into this advanced outline.

Try this exercise: imagine a line drawn from the point of the horse's hip, through the point of shoulder to his chin. Lunge the horse and keep him balanced by maintaining his position on this imaginary line. You will notice he automatically distributes more weight on his quarters, lightens his forehand and his gaits become more expressive.

If his chin drops below this line it tends to move the horse forwards but also downwards. This plops him onto his forehand and 'free wheels' him on his hindquarters. You may mistakenly believe he is engaged when, in fact, he is avoiding taking the weight over the hind legs.

The modern trend of loosening the horse

with his head and neck 'long and deep' has many benefits and many dangers. Balanced lungeing works the same muscles as the 'long and deep' method but, because the horse is working in self-carriage, the negative effects of dumping the horse on his forehand do not occur.

The purpose of balanced lungeing is to say, 'I'm the trainer, I'm the balance and I want to be able to bring the horse's hocks more under his body and lighten his forehand.'

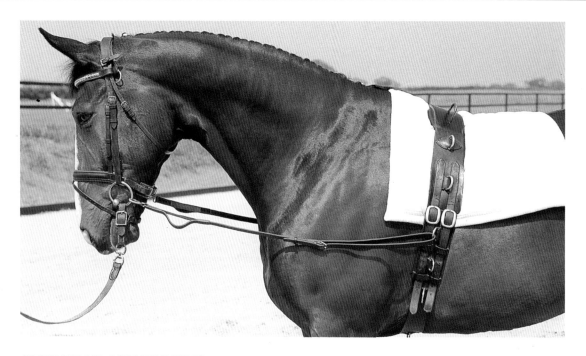

OVERHEAD CHECK REINS

These stop the horse from leaning on the bit or from coming behind the vertical. The head piece is the de Gogue head piece which consists of a band of leather with rings attached. Place the head piece under the bridle browband and buckle the small straps on the de Gogue to the head piece of the bridle. It should fit comfortably behind the horse's ears and not be too tight or pulled forwards.

The overhead check reins are approximately 1.8 m (6 ft) long. They clip to the snaffle rings, run through the rings on the head piece and onto a strap fastened to the top D ring on the roller. This strap lies about two hands' length in front of the wither.

PAUL'S TIP

Be wary of the dangers of overbending the horse. The horse should be seeking the bit. When the horse's head comes behind the vertical he is overbent. If you imagine a vertical line drawn from the horse's poll down through his nose to the ground and his nose comes behind this line, you know he is behind the vertical. As an approximate guide, work the novice horse so that he holds his head 5–10 per cent in front of the vertical, and an advanced horse 0–5 per cent.

LUNGEING TO EDUCATE

The skilled trainer understands when to put the pressure on a horse and when to take the pressure off. For example, the educated hand maintains the horse's balance. Sympathetically this hand instructs and frames the horse, it gives the contact when the horse gives a better feel on the reins and rebalances him when he takes too much weight on the reins. The trainer is being proactive and not reactive.

Progress your trainer skills by harmonizing with the horse and, particularly, avoiding conflicts. These can arise because you are making too severe demands on the horse. Go with his natural energy and gradually build on it by developing his muscles and fitness. Once you have reached a reasonable level of harmony there will be times when you should take a more passive role and allow the horse to continue his work without interference. This period of time is called 'conditioning the horse'. It is important because it promotes submission, confidence and strength in the horse.

PAUL'S TIP

Always wear gloves. They will prevent rope burns should the horse pull the rein through your hands.

Half halts Half halts contain the energy of the horse. The trainer re-directs some of the forwardness back to the hindquarters. He asks the horse for more engagement. Initially, use voice commands. This encourages the horse to understand the half-halt aids more easily.

Transitions Transitions improve the activity, gaits and balance of the horse. Lunge the horse in frequent transitions from trot to walk and canter to trot. Check that the horse moves briskly forwards to the forward aids and reacts to the half halts. Ensure he steps more 'up and under' with his hindquarters in the downward transitions. Initially, ask for progressive transitions but when the horse develops in strength, make the transitions more frequent and more demanding.

Centre of gravity Your aim is to shift the centre of gravity so that the horse's weight is distributed more on his hindquarters and less on his forehand.

The first stage is to supple the horse so that he stretches along his top line and seeks the bit. In the working gaits his hind legs step more forward and under his body and, at each step, he strides over his own centre of gravity

which, for a dressage horse, runs in a line from behind the wither to the ground. (At this stage the horse is in 50–50 equilibrium, opposite, top).

The second stage is to lighten the forehand. Transitions and half halts have prepared him for this by directing his energy back towards his hindquarters. (The same horse in 60–40 equilibrium, below).

GEARING FOR ENGAGEMENT

The 'Harmonizer' increases engagement without the trainer urging the horse forwards too much and possibly, in some instances, upsetting his balance. The bridging strap copies the actions of long reins and offers you a safe and easy method of introducing the horse to two reins.

The bridging strap hangs above the horse's hocks and encases his hindquarters. A strap with rubber inserts links the bridging strap to the reins, these pass through the D rings, through the bit rings and then return to the roller. The bridging strap gently nudges the horse forwards into greater engagement by gently making contact with the horse at every stride.

TOWARDS COLLECTION

Start by trotting the horse on the lunge and spiral him to follow the line of a 20 m circle down to a 10 m circle. The effect is similar to shoulder-fore, the horse transfers and loads more weight onto his hindquarters. Be careful to maintain the forwardness, this exercise can have a tendency to reduce tempo and 'takt' (rhythm). Make sure the horse tracks up evenly and energetically, i.e. you can see the hind hooves step into or over his front hoof prints.

TOWARDS EXTENSION

Encourage the horse's working trot into a lengthened trot, for about seven to eight strides, by lungeing him off an oval-shaped circle and onto a straight line. Return to an oval-shaped circle at the end of the first straight line and then repeat the lengthened strides on another straight line. Once he can perform this new exercise easily, you can encourage the horse to work more actively through his lengthened trot strides into a medium trot.

Be patient if your horse breaks into canter. Send him forward into trot, maintaining a light feel on the lunge rein. Push him forwards through this misunderstanding and soon he will know you really wanted medium trot and not canter.

The photograph below shows a horse in medium trot. The overhead check reins and the side reins, which are fitted high on the roller, help maintain self-carriage and encourage the horse to move 'uphill' in balance.

ACKNOWLEDGEMENTS

Thank you to Tessa Fielder for appearing in some of the photographs and thank you to the groom, Maxine Spalding, for her hard work and enthusiasm. A special thank you to the Belgian gelding, Broadland Optimist (Sire: King Darco, Dam: Eveline).

British Library Cataloguing-in-Publication Data.
A catalogue record for this book is available from the
British Library

ISBN 0.85131.732.4

Published in Great Britain in 1999 by
J. A. Allen an imprint of Robert Hale Ltd.,
Clerkenwell House, 45–47 Clerkenwell Green,
London EC1R 0HT

Design and Typesetting by Paul Saunders
Series editor Jane Lake
Printed in Hong Kong by Dah Hua Printing Press Co. Ltd.